Title: My First Healthy Habits Book

Published by Wise Oyster

Library of Congress Control Number:

Hardcover ISBN: 9781662917875

My First
Healthy Habits Book

This book belongs to

Wise Oyster

Author **Maria Christina Gigante**

Illustrator **Vika Samsonova**

Always remember, health is a commitment of what we do every single day. The ability to create a beautiful, happy, and healthy life is in your hands.

The world is your oyster.

Love,
Maria

"Tell me and I forget.
Teach me and I remember.
Involve me and I learn."

Benjamin Franklin

Dedication

Dedicated to the next generation of children. May you learn how to respect and honor your body and never underestimate the joy of simple pleasures in daily life.

And to their parents and guardians for choosing to instill the value of daily habits and to grow healthy together as a family.

How to use this book

This book can be used as a verbalized journal to recap the day before bedtime. It promotes healthy conversation between the family member and child about daily habits for living a fun and healthy life.

Children are taught by example and when habits are created together, they are more easily able to manifest in life. Creating foundational habits for a healthy life begins in childhood and lasts a lifetime.

Foundational Daily Habits:

Music

Laughter

Sleep

Sun

Colorful Foods

Hydration

Breath

Gratitude

Movement

Good morning! The sun is shining!

The bright sun wakes me up and tells me to enjoy my day. What were the colors of your sunrise today?

I love to drink water!

It refreshes me and keeps me hydrated throughout my day.

How much water did you drink today?

Playing outside in nature
makes me happy.

Sometimes I play in the snow...

and other times I swim
in the ocean!

What games did you
play outside today?

When I see my friends, we always laugh together.
I love laughing with them! What made you laugh today?

I love to eat colorful food

so I get nutrients in my body

to give me energy!

I love to eat blueberries, strawberries, eggs, and peas. These are just a few of my favorite foods! How many colors did you eat today?

Sometimes when things don't go my way,

I sit down and take in a deep breath all the way down

to my belly and remember the things I am grateful for.

What are some of the things you are grateful for?

When I play music, it makes me feel happy and peaceful.

It makes me dance and sing.
What songs did you listen to today?

When the moon and stars come out
at night, I know it's time for bed.
Sometimes when I look up
to the sky, I see a shooting star.

Then I wash my face, brush my teeth,
and get comfortable under my blanket.
Are you comfy in your bed tonight?

Author Bio

Maria Gigante, MS, CNS, CDN, LDN is a Nutritionist and Holistic Lifestyle Coach. She is a first-generation Italian American.

Her parents and grandparents immigrated to the USA in the 1970s. She and her younger brother were born and raised in Jersey City, New Jersey. Maria's early childhood was spent in her grandmother's kitchen, cooking and eating food from her grandparents' tiny city garden and listening to Italian folk music while recounting stories of when her grandparents grew up during WWII in Ortona A Mare, Abruzzo, Italy.

Maria's traditional upbringing in a diverse city has molded her perspective on the importance of culture, lifestyle, and nutrition. She is fluent in English, Italian, and Spanish. She also enjoys family time, preparing nourishing meals, fashion, swimming, hiking, music, and dancing.

Lightning Source UK Ltd.
Milton Keynes UK
UKHW050933080622
404071UK00002B/100

9 781662 917875